DUTCHMAN

DUTCHMAN

a play by LeRoi Jones

FABER AND FABER
24 Russell Square London

First published in England in mcmlxv
by Faber and Faber Limited
24 Russell Square, London WC1
First published in this edition mcmlxvii
Printed in Great Britain by
Lowe & Brydone (Printers) Ltd., London

‧

ᘜ **1 2 NOV 1969**

For Thomas Everett Russ, American pioneer,
and Anna Cherry Brock Russ, his wife

DUTCHMAN

Characters

C L A Y , twenty-year-old Negro

L U L A , thirty-year-old white woman

R I D E R S   O F   C O A C H , white and black

Y O U N G   N E G R O

C O N D U C T O R

In the flying underbelly of the city. Steaming hot, and summer on top, outside. Underground. The subway heaped in modern myth.

Opening scene is a man sitting in a subway seat, holding a magazine but looking vacantly just above its wilting pages. Occasionally he looks blankly toward the window on his right. Dim lights and darkness whistling by against the glass. (Or paste the lights, as admitted props, right on the subway windows. Have them move, even dim and flicker. But give the sense of speed. Also stations, whether the train is stopped or the glitter and activity of these stations merely flashes by the windows.)

The man is sitting alone. That is, only his seat is visible, though the rest of the car is outfitted as a complete subway car. But only his seat is shown. There might be, for a time, as the play begins, a loud scream of the actual train. And it can recur throughout the play, or continue on a lower key once the dialogue starts.

The train slows after a time, pulling to a brief stop at one of the stations. The man looks idly up, until he sees a woman's face staring at him through the window; when it realizes that the man has noticed the face, it begins very premeditatedly to smile. The man smiles too, for a moment, without a trace of self-consciousness. Almost an instinctive though undesirable response. Then a kind of awkwardness or embarrassment sets in, and the man makes to look away, is further embarrassed, so he brings back his eyes to where the face was, but by now the train is moving again, and the face would seem to be left behind by the way the man turns his head to look back through the other windows at the slowly fading platform. He smiles then; more comfortably confident, hoping perhaps that his memory of this brief encounter will be pleasant. And then he is idle again.

Scene I

Train roars. Lights flash outside the windows.

LULA *enters from the rear of the car in bright, skimpy summer clothes and sandals. She carries a net bag full of paper books, fruit, and other anonymous articles. She is wearing sunglasses, which she pushes up on her forehead from time to time.* LULA *is a tall, slender, beautiful woman with long red hair hanging straight down her back, wearing only loud lipstick in somebody's good taste. She is eating an apple, very daintily. Coming down the car toward* CLAY.

She stops beside CLAY'*s seat and hangs languidly from the strap, still managing to eat the apple. It is apparent that she is going to sit in the seat next to* CLAY, *and that she is only waiting for him to notice her before she sits.*

CLAY *sits as before, looking just beyond his magazine, now and again pulling the magazine slowly back and forth in front of his face in a hopeless effort to fan himself. Then he sees the woman hanging there beside him and he looks up into her face, smiling quizzically.*

LULA. Hello.

CLAY. Uh, hi're you?

LULA. I'm going to sit down. . . . O.K.?

CLAY. Sure.

LULA.
[*Swings down onto the seat, pushing her legs straight out as if she is very weary*]
Oooof! Too much weight.

CLAY. Ha, doesn't look like much to me.
[*Leaning back against the window, a little surprised and maybe stiff*]

LULA. It's so anyway.
[*And she moves her toes in the sandals, then pulls her right leg up on the left knee, better to inspect the bottoms of the sandals and the back of her heel. She appears for a second not to notice that* CLAY *is sitting next to her or that she has spoken to him just a second before.* CLAY *looks at the magazine, then out the black window. As he does this, she turns very quickly toward him*]
Weren't you staring at me through the window?

CLAY.
[*Wheeling around and very much stiffened*]
What?

LULA. Weren't you staring at me through the window? At the last stop?

CLAY. Staring at you? What do you mean?

LULA. Don't you know what staring means?

CLAY. I saw you through the window . . . if that's what

it means. I don't know if I was staring. Seems to me you were staring through the window at me.

LULA. I was. But only after I'd turned around and saw you staring through that window down in the vicinity of my ass and legs.

CLAY. Really?

LULA. Really. I guess you were just taking those idle pot-shots. Nothing else to do. Run your mind over people's flesh.

CLAY. Oh boy. Wow, now I admit I was looking in your direction. But the rest of that weight is yours.

LULA. I suppose.

CLAY. Staring through train windows is weird business. Much weirder than staring very sedately at abstract asses.

LULA. That's why I came looking through the window . . . so you'd have more than that to go on. I even smiled at you.

CLAY. That's right.

LULA. I even got into this train, going some other way than mine. Walked down the aisle . . . searching you out.

CLAY. Really? That's pretty funny.

LULA. That's pretty funny. . . . God, you're dull.

CLAY. Well, I'm sorry, lady, but I really wasn't prepared for party talk.

LULA. No, you're not. What are you prepared for?
[*Wrapping the apple core in a Kleenex and dropping it on the floor*]

CLAY.
[*Takes her conversation as pure sex talk. He turns to confront her squarely with this idea*]
I'm prepared for anything. How about you?

LULA.
[*Laughing loudly and cutting it off abruptly*]
What do you think you're doing?

CLAY. What?

LULA. You think I want to pick you up, get you to take me somewhere and screw me, huh?

CLAY. Is that the way I look?

LULA. You look like you been trying to grow a beard. That's exactly what you look like. You look like you live in New Jersey with your parents and are trying to grow a beard. That's what. You look like you've been reading Chinese poetry and drinking lukewarm sugarless tea.
[*Laughs, uncrossing and recrossing her legs*]
You look like death eating a soda cracker.

CLAY.

[*Cocking his head from one side to the other, embarrassed and trying to make some comeback, but also intrigued by what the woman is saying . . . even the sharp city coarseness of her voice, which is still a kind of gentle sidewalk throb*]

Really? I look like all that?

LULA. Not all of it.

[*She feints a seriousness to cover an actual somber tone*]

I lie a lot.

[*Smiling*]

It helps me control the world.

CLAY.

[*Relieved and laughing louder than the humor*]

Yeah, I bet.

LULA. But it's true, most of it, right? Jersey? Your bumpy neck?

CLAY. How'd you know all that? Huh? Really, I mean about Jersey . . . and even the beard. I met you before? You know Warren Enright?

LULA. You tried to make it with your sister when you were ten.

[CLAY *leanes back hard against the back of the seat, his eyes opening now, still trying to look amused*]

But I succeeded a few weeks ago.

[*She starts to laugh again*]

CLAY. What're you talking about? Warren tell you that? You're a friend of Georgia's?

LULA. I told you I lie. I don't know your sister. I don't know Warren Enright.

CLAY. You mean you're just picking these things out of the air?

LULA. Is Warren Enright a tall skinny black black boy with a phony English accent?

CLAY. I figured you knew him.

LULA. But I don't. I just figured you would know somebody like that.
[*Laughs*]

CLAY. Yeah, yeah.

LULA. You're probably on your way to his house now.

CLAY. That's right.

LULA.
[*Putting her hand on Clay's closest knee, drawing it from the knee up to the thigh's hinge, then removing it, watching his face very closely, and continuing to laugh, perhaps more gently than before*]
Dull, dull, dull. I bet you think I'm exciting.

CLAY. You're O.K.

LULA. Am I exciting you now?

CLAY. Right. That's not what's supposed to happen?

LULA. How do I know?

> [*She returns her hand, without moving it, then takes it away and plunges it in her bag to draw out an apple*]

You want this?

CLAY. Sure.

LULA.

> [*She gets one out of the bag for herself*]

Eating apples together is always the first step. Or walking up uninhabited Seventh Avenue in the twenties on week-ends.

> [*Bites and giggles, glancing at Clay and speaking in loose sing-song*]

Can get you involved . . . boy! Get us involved. Um-huh.

> [*Mock seriousness*]

Would you like to get involved with me, Mister Man?

CLAY.

> [*Trying to be as flippant as Lula, whacking happily at the apple*]

Sure. Why not? A beautiful woman like you. Huh, I'd be a fool not to.

LULA. And I bet you're sure you know what you're talking about.

> [*Taking him a little roughly by the wrist, so he cannot eat the apple, then shaking the wrist*]

I bet you're sure of almost everything anybody ever asked you about . . . right?

> [*Shakes his wrist harder*]

Right?

B

CLAY. Yeah, right. . . . Wow, you're pretty strong, you know? Whatta you, a lady wrestler or something?

LULA. What's wrong with lady wrestlers? And don't answer because you never knew any. Huh.
[*Cynically*]
That's for sure. They don't have any lady wrestlers in that part of Jersey. That's for sure.

CLAY. Hey, you still haven't told me how you know so much about me.

LULA. I told you I didn't know anything about *you* . . . you're a well-known type.

CLAY. Really?

LULA. Or at least I know the type very well. And your skinny English friend too.

CLAY. Anonymously?

LULA.
[*Settles back in seat, single-mindedly finishing her apple and humming snatches of rhythm and blues song*]
What?

CLAY. Without knowing us specifically?

LULA. Oh boy.
[*Looking quickly at Clay*]
What a face. You know, you could be a handsome man.

CLAY. I can't argue with you.

LULA.
[*Vague, off-center response*]
What?

CLAY.
[*Raising his voice, thinking the train noise has drowned part of his sentence*]
I can't argue with you.

LULA. My hair is turning gray. A gray hair for each year and type I've come through.

CLAY. Why do you want to sound so old?

LULA. But it's always gentle when it starts.
[*Attention drifting*]
Hugged against tenements, day or night.

CLAY. What?

LULA.
[*Refocusing*]
Hey, why don't you take me to that party you're going to?

CLAY. You must be a friend of Warren's to know about the party.

LULA. Wouldn't you like to take me to the party?
[*Imitates clinging vine*]
Oh, come on, ask me to your party.

CLAY. Of course I'll ask you to come with me to the party. And I'll bet you're a friend of Warren's.

LULA. Why not be a friend of Warren's? Why not?
   [*Taking his arm*]
Have you asked me yet?

CLAY. How can I ask you when I don't know your name?

LULA. Are you talking to my name?

CLAY. What is it, a secret?

LULA. I'm Lena the Hyena.

CLAY. The famous woman poet?

LULA. Poetess! The same!

CLAY. Well, you know so much about me . . . what's my name?

LULA. Morris the Hyena.

CLAY. The famous woman poet?

LULA. The same.
   [*Laughing and going into her bag*]
You want another apple?

CLAY. Can't make it, lady. I only have to keep one doctor away a day.

LULA. I bet your name is . . . something like . . . uh, Gerald or Walter. Huh?

CLAY. God, no.

LULA. Lloyd, Norman? One of those hopeless colored names creeping out of New Jersey. Leonard? Gag. . . .

CLAY. Like Warren?

LULA. Definitely. Just exactly like Warren. Or Everett.

CLAY. Gag. . . .

LULA. Well, for sure, it's not Willie.

CLAY. It's Clay.

LULA. Clay? Really? Clay what?

CLAY. Take your pick. Jackson, Johnson, or Williams.

LULA. Oh, really? Good for you. But it's got to be Williams. You're too pretentious to be a Jackson or Johnson.

CLAY. Thass right.

LULA. But Clay's O.K.

CLAY. So's Lena.

LULA. It's Lula.

CLAY. Oh?

LULA. Lula the Hyena.

CLAY. Very good.

LULA.
   [Starts laughing again]
Now you say to me, "Lula, Lula, why don't you go to this
party with me tonight?" It's your turn, and let those be
your lines.

CLAY. Lula, why don't you go to this party with me tonight, Huh?

LULA. Say my name twice before you ask, and no huh's.

CLAY. Lula, Lula, why don't you go to this party with me
tonight?

LULA. I'd like to go, Clay, but how can you ask me to go
when you barely know me?

CLAY. That is strange, isn't it?

LULA. What kind of reaction is that? You're supposed to
say, "Aw, come on, we'll get to know each other better at
the party."

CLAY. That's pretty corny.

LULA. What are you into anyway?

[*Looking at him half sullenly but still amused*]
What thing are you playing at, Mister? Mister Clay Williams?
[*Grabs his thigh, up near the crotch*]
What are *you* thinking about?

CLAY. Watch it now, you're gonna excite me for real.

LULA.
[*Taking her hand away and throwing her apple core through the window*]
I bet.
[*She slumps in the seat and is heavily silent*]

CLAY. I thought you knew everything about me? What happened?
[LULA *looks at him, then looks slowly away, then over where the other aisle would be. Noise of the train. She reaches in her bag and pulls out one of the paper books. She puts it on her leg and thumbs the pages listlessly.* CLAY *cocks his head to see the title of the book. Noise of the train.* LULA *flips pages and her eyes drift. Both remain silent*]
Are you going to the party with me, Lula?

LULA.
[*Bored and not even looking*]
I don't even know you.

CLAY. You said you know my type.

LULA.
[*Strangely irritated*]
Don't get smart with me, Buster. I know you like the palm of my hand.

CLAY. The one you eat the apples with?

LULA. Yeh. And the one I open doors late Saturday evening with. That's my door. Up at the top of the stairs. Five flights. Above a lot of Italians and lying Americans. And scrape carrots with. Also . . .
[*Looks at him*]
the same hand I unbutton my dress with, or let my skirt fall down. Same hand. Lover.

CLAY. Are you angry about anything? Did I say something wrong?

LULA. Everything you say is wrong.
[*Mock smile*]
That's what makes you so attractive. Ha. In that funnybook jacket with all the buttons.
[*More animate, taking hold of his jacket*]
What've you got that jacket and tie on in all this heat for? And why're you wearing a jacket and tie like that? Did your people ever burn witches or start revolutions over the price of tea? Boy, those narrow-shoulder clothes come from a tradition you ought to feel oppressed by. A three-button suit. What right do you have to be wearing a three-button suit and striped tie? Your grandfather was a slave, he didn't go to Harvard.

CLAY. My grandfather was a night watchman.

LULA. And you went to a colored college where everybody thought they were Averell Harriman.

CLAY. All except me.

LULA. And who did you think you were? Who do you think you are now?

CLAY.
[*Laughs as if to make light of the whole trend of the conversation*]
Well, in college I thought I was Baudelaire. But I've slowed down since.

LULA. I bet you never once thought you were a black nigger.
[*Mock serious, then she howls with laughter.* CLAY *is stunned but after initial reaction, he quickly tries to appreciate the humor.* LULA *almost shrieks*]
A black Baudelaire.

CLAY. That's right.

LULA. Boy, are you corny. I take back what I said before. Everything you say is not wrong. It's perfect. You should be on television.

CLAY. You act like you're on television already.

LULA. That's because I'm an actress.

CLAY. I thought so.

LULA. Well, you're wrong. I'm no actress. I told you I always lie. I'm nothing, honey, and don't you ever forget it.
[*Lighter*]
Although my mother was a Communist. The only person in my family ever to amount to anything.

CLAY. My mother was a Republican.

LULA. And your father voted for the man rather than the party.

CLAY. Right!

LULA. Yea for him. Yea, yea for him.

CLAY. Yea!

LULA. And yea for America where he is free to vote for the mediocrity of his choice! Yea!

CLAY. Yea!

LULA. And yea for both your parents who even though they differ about so crucial a matter as the body politic still forged a union of love and sacrifice that was destined to flower at the birth of the noble Clay . . . what's your middle name?

CLAY. Clay.

LULA. A union of love and sacrifice that was destined to flower at the birth of the noble Clay Clay Williams. Yea! And most of all yea yea for you, Clay Clay. The Black Baudelaire! Yes!
    [*And with knifelike cynicism*]
My Christ. My Christ.

CLAY. Thank you, ma'am.

LULA. May the people accept you as a ghost of the future. And love you, that you might not kill them when you can.

CLAY. What?

LULA. You're a murderer, Clay, and you know it.
    [*Her voice darkening with significance*]
You know goddamn well what I mean.

CLAY. I do?

LULA. So we'll pretend the air is light and full of perfume.

CLAY.
    [*Sniffing at her blouse*]
It is.

LULA. And we'll pretend the people cannot see you. That is, the citizens. And that you are free of your own history. And I am free of my history. We'll pretend that we are both anonymous beauties smashing along through the city's entrails.
    [*She yells as loud as she can*]
GROOVE!

Black

Scene II

Scene is the same as before, though now there are other seats visible in the car. And throughout the scene other people get on the subway. There are maybe one or two seated in the car as the scene opens, though neither CLAY *nor* LULA *notices them.* CLAY's *tie is open.* LULA *is hugging his arm.*

CLAY. The party!

LULA. I know it'll be something good. You can come in with me, looking casual and significant. I'll be strange, haughty, and silent, and walk with long slow strides.

CLAY. Right.

LULA. When you get drunk, pat me once, very lovingly on the flanks, and I'll look at you cryptically, licking my lips.

CLAY. It sounds like something we can do.

LULA. You'll go around talking to young men about your mind, and to old men about your plans. If you meet a very close friend who is also with someone like me, we can stand together, sipping our drinks and exchanging codes of lust. The atmosphere will be slithering in love and half-love and very open moral decision.

CLAY. Great. Great.

LULA. And everyone will pretend they don't know your name, and then . . .
   [*She pauses heavily*]
later, when they have to, they'll claim a friendship that denies your sterling character.

CLAY.
   [*Kissing her neck and fingers*]
And then what?

LULA. Then? Well, then we'll go down the street, late night, eating apples and winding very deliberately toward my house.

CLAY. Deliberately?

LULA. I mean, we'll look in all the shopwindows, and make fun of the queers. Maybe we'll meet a Jewish Buddhist and flatten his conceits over some very pretentious coffee.

CLAY. In honor of whose God?

LULA. Mine.

CLAY. Who is . . . ?

LULA. Me . . . and you?

CLAY. A corporate Godhead.

LULA. Exactly. Exactly.
   [*Notices one of the other people entering*]

CLAY. Go on with the chronicle. Then what happens to us?

LULA.
   [*A mild depression, but she still makes her description trium-
   phant and increasingly direct*]
To my house, of course.

CLAY. Of course.

LULA. And up the narrow steps of the tenement.

CLAY. You live in a tenement?

LULA. Wouldn't live anywhere else. Reminds me specifically of my novel form of insanity.

CLAY. Up the tenement stairs.

LULA. And with my apple-eating hand I push open the door
and lead you, my tender big-eyed prey, into my . . . God,
what can I call it . . . into my hovel.

CLAY. Then what happens?

LULA. After the dancing and games, after the long drinks
and long walks, the real fun begins.

CLAY. Ah, the real fun.
> [*Embarrassed, in spite of himself*]

Which is . . . ?

LULA.
> [*Laughs at him*]

Real fun in the dark house. Hah! Real fun in the dark house, high up above the street and the ignorant cowboys. I lead you in, holding your wet hand gently in my hand . . .

CLAY. Which is not wet?

LULA. Which is dry as ashes.

CLAY. And cold?

LULA. Don't think you'll get out of your responsibility that way. It's not cold at all. You Fascist! Into my dark living room. Where we'll sit and talk endlessly, endlessly.

CLAY. About what?

LULA. About what? About your manhood, what do you think? What do you think we've been talking about all this time?

CLAY. Well, I didn't know it was that. That's for sure. Every other thing in the world but that.
> [*Notices another person entering, looks quickly, almost involuntarily up and down the car, seeing the other people in the car*]

Hey, I didn't even notice when those people got on.

LULA. Yeah, I know.

CLAY. Man, this subway is slow.

LULA. Yeah, I know.

CLAY. Well, go on. We were talking about my manhood.

LULA. We still are. All the time.

CLAY. We were in your living room.

LULA. My dark living room. Talking endlessly.

CLAY. About my manhood.

LULA. I'll make you a map of it. Just as soon as we get to my house.

CLAY. Well, that's great.

LULA. One of the things we do while we talk. And screw.

CLAY.
    [*Trying to make his smile broader and less shaky*]
We finally got there.

LULA. And you'll call my rooms black as a grave. You'll say, "This place is like Juliet's tomb."

CLAY.
    [*Laughs*]
I might.

LULA. I know. You've probably said it before.

CLAY. And is that all? The whole grand tour?

LULA. Not all. You'll say to me very close to my face, many, many times, you'll say, even whisper, that you love me.

CLAY. Maybe I will.

LULA. And you'll be lying.

CLAY. I wouldn't lie about something like that.

LULA. Hah. It's the only kind of thing you will lie about. Especially if you think it'll keep me alive.

CLAY. Keep you alive? I don't understand.

LULA.
   [*Bursting out laughing, but too shrilly*]
Don't understand? Well, don't look at me. It's the path I take, that's all. Where both feet take me when I set them down. One in front of the other.

CLAY. Morbid. Morbid. You sure you're not an actress? All that self-aggrandizement.

LULA. Well, I told you I wasn't an actress . . . but I also told you I lie all the time. Draw your own conclusions.

CLAY. Morbid. Morbid. You sure you're not an actress? All scribed? There's no more?

C

LULA. I've told you all I know. Or almost all.

CLAY. There's no funny parts?

LULA. I thought it was all funny.

CLAY. But you mean peculiar, not ha-ha.

LULA. You don't know what I mean.

CLAY. Well, tell me the almost part then. You said almost all. What else? I want the whole story.

LULA.

  [*Searching aimlessly through her bag. She begins to talk breathlessly, with a light and silly tone*]

All stories are whole stories. All of 'em. Our whole story . . . nothing but change. How could things go on like that forever? Huh?

  [*Slaps him on the shoulder, begins finding things in her bag, taking them out and throwing them over her shoulder into the aisle*]

Except I do go on as I do. Apples and long walks with deathless intelligent lovers. But you mix it up. Look out the window, all the time. Turning pages. Change change change. Till, shit, I don't know you. Wouldn't, for that matter. You're too serious. I bet you're even too serious to be psychoanalyzed. Like all those Jewish poets from Yonkers, who leave their mothers looking for other mothers, or others' mothers, on whose baggy tits they lay their fumbling heads. Their poems are always funny, and all about sex.

CLAY. They sound great. Like movies.

LULA. But you change.
> [*Blankly*]
And things work on you till you hate them.
> [*More people come into the train. They come closer to the couple, some of them not sitting, but swinging drearily on the straps, staring at the two with uncertain interest*]

CLAY. Wow. All these people, so suddenly. They must all come from the same place.

LULA. Right. That they do.

CLAY. Oh? You know about them too?

LULA. Oh yeah. About them more than I know about you. Do they frighten you?

CLAY. Frighten me? Why should they frighten me?

LULA. 'Cause you're an escaped nigger.

CLAY. Yeah?

LULA. 'Cause you crawled through the wire and made tracks to my side.

CLAY. Wire?

LULA. Don't they have wire around plantations?

CLAY. You must be Jewish. All you can think about is wire. Plantations didn't have any wire. Plantations were big open whitewashed places like heaven, and everybody on 'em was grooved to be there. Just strummin' and hummin' all day.

LULA. Yes, yes.

CLAY. And that's how the blues was born.

LULA. Yes, yes. And that's how the blues was born.
[*Begins to make up a song that becomes quickly hysterical. As she sings she rises from her seat, still throwing things out of her bag into the aisle, beginning a rhythmical shudder and twistlike wiggle, which she continues up and down the aisle, bumping into many of the standing people and tripping over the feet of those sitting. Each time she runs into a person she lets out a very vicious piece of profanity, wiggling and step-ing all the time*]
And that's how the blues was born. Yes. Yes. Son of a bitch, get out of the way. Yes. Quack. Yes. Yes. And that's how the blues was born. Ten little niggers sitting on a limb, but none of them ever looked like him.
[*Points to* CLAY, *returns toward the seat, with her hands ex-tended for him to rise and dance with her*]
And that's how blues was born. Yes. Come on, Clay. Let's do the nasty. Rub bellies. Rub bellies.

CLAY.
[*Waves his hands to refuse. He is embarrassed, but deter-mined to get a kick out of the proceedings*]
Hey, what was in those apples? Mirror, mirror on the wall, who's the fairest one of all? Snow White, baby, and don't you forget it.

LULA.
[*Grabbing for his hands, which he draws away*]

Come on, Clay. Let's rub bellies on the train. The nasty. The nasty. Do the gritty grind, like your ol' rag-head mammy. Grind till you lose your mind. Shake it, shake it, shake it, shake it! OOOOweeee! Come on, Clay. Let's do the choo-choo train shuffle, the navel scratcher.

CLAY. Hey, you coming on like the lady who smoked up her grass skirt.

LULA.
   [*Becoming annoyed that he will not dance, and becoming more animated as if to embarrass him still further*]
Come on, Clay . . . let's do the thing. Uhh! Uhh! Clay! Clay! You middle-class black bastard. Forget your social-working mother for a few seconds and let's knock stomachs. Clay, you liver-lipped white man. You would-be Christian. You ain't no nigger, you're just a dirty white man. Get up, Clay. Dance with me, Clay.

CLAY. Lula! Sit down, now. Be cool.

LULA.
   [*Mocking him, in wild dance*]
Be cool. Be cool. That's all you know . . . shaking that wildroot cream-oil on your knotty head, jackets buttoning up to your chin, so full of white man's words. Christ. God. Get up and scream at these people. Like scream meaningless shit in these hopeless faces.
   [*She screams at people in train, still dancing*]
Red trains cough Jewish underwear for keeps! Expanding smells of silence. Gravy snot whistling like sea birds. Clay. Clay, you got to break out. Don't sit there dying the way they want you to die. Get up.

CLAY. Oh, sit the fuck down.

> [*He moves to restrain her*]

Sit down, goddamn it.

LULA.

> [*Twisting out of his reach*]

Screw yourself, Uncle Tom. Thomas Woolly-head.

> [*Begins to dance a kind of jig, mocking Clay with loud forced humor*]

There is Uncle Tom . . . I mean, Uncle Thomas Woolly-Head. With old white matted mane. He hobbles on his wooden cane. Old Tom. Old Tom. Let the white man hump his ol' mama, and he jes' shuffle off in the woods and hide his gentle gray head. Ol' Thomas Woolly-Head.

> [*Some of the other riders are laughing now. A drunk gets up and joins* LULA *in her dance, singing, as best he can, her "song."* CLAY *gets up out of his seat and visibly scans the faces of the other riders*]

CLAY. Lula! Lula!

> [*She is dancing and turning, still shouting as loud as she can. The drunk too is shouting, and waving his hands wildly*]

Lula . . . you dumb bitch. Why don't you stop it?

> [*He rushes half stumbling from his seat, and grabs one of her flailing arms*]

LULA. Let me go! You black son of a bitch.

> [*She struggles against him*]

Let me go! Help!

> [CLAY *is dragging her towards her seat, and the drunk seeks to interfere. He grabs* CLAY *around the shoulders and begins wrestling with him.* CLAY *clubs the drunk to the floor without releasing* LULA, *who is still screaming.* CLAY *finally gets her to the seat and throws her into it*]

CLAY. Now you shut the hell up.

> [*Grabbing her shoulders*]

Just shut up. You don't know what you're talking about. You don't know anything. So just keep your stupid mouth closed.

LULA. You're afraid of white people. And your father was. Uncle Tom Big Lip!

CLAY.

> [*Slaps her as hard as he can, across the mouth.* LULA's *head bangs against the back of the seat. When she raises it again,* CLAY *slaps her again*]

Now shut up and let me talk.

> [*He turns toward the other riders, some of whom are sitting on the edge of their seats. The drunk is on one knee, rubbing his head, and singing softly the same song. He shuts up too when he sees* CLAY *watching him. The others go back to newspapers or stare out the windows*]

Shit, you don't have any sense, Lula, nor feelings either. I could murder you now. Such a tiny ugly throat. I could squeeze it flat, and watch you turn blue, on a humble. For dull kicks. And all these weak-faced ofays squatting around here, staring over their papers at me. Murder them too. Even if they expected it. That man there . . .

> [*Points to well-dressed man*]

I could rip that *Times* right out of his hand, as skinny and middle-classed as I am, I could rip that paper out of his hand and just as easily rip out his throat. It takes no great effort. For what? To kill you soft idiots? You don't understand anything but luxury.

LULA. You fool!

CLAY.

[*Pushing her against the seat*]

I'm not telling you again, Tallulah Bankhead! Luxury. In your face and your fingers. You telling me what I ought to do.

[*Sudden scream frightening the whole coach*]

Well, don't! Don't you tell me anything! If I'm a middle-class fake white man . . . let me be. And let me be in the way I want.

[*Through his teeth*]

I'll rip your lousy breasts off! Let me be who I feel like being. Uncle Tom. Thomas. Whoever. It's none of your business. You don't know anything except what's there for you to see. An act. Lies. Device. Not the pure heart, the pumping black heart. You don't ever know that. And I sit here, in this buttoned-up suit, to keep myself from cutting all your throats. I mean wantonly. You great liberated whore! You fuck some black man, and right away you're an expert on black people. What a lotta shit that is. The only thing you know is that you come if he bangs you hard enough. And that's all. The belly rub? You wanted to do the belly rub? Shit, you don't even know how. You don't know how. That ol' dipty-dip shit you do, rolling your ass like an elephant. That's not my kind of belly rub. Belly rub is not Queens. Belly rub is dark places, with big hats and overcoats held up with one arm. Belly rub hates you. Old bald-headed four-eyed ofays popping their fingers . . . and don't know yet what they're doing. They say, "I love Bessie Smith." And don't even understand that Bessie Smith is saying, "Kiss my ass, kiss my black unruly ass." Before love, suffering, desire, anything you can explain, she's saying, and very plainly, "Kiss my black ass." And if you don't know that, it's you that's doing the kissing.

Charlie Parker? Charlie Parker. All the hip white boys scream for Bird. And Bird saying, "Up your ass, feeble-minded ofay! Up your ass." And they sit there talking about the tortured genius of Charlie Parker. Bird would've played not a note of music if he just walked up to East Sixty-seventh Street and killed the first ten white people he saw. Not a note! And I'm the great would-be poet. Yes. That's right! Poet. Some kind of bastard literature . . . all it needs is a simple knife thrust. Just let me bleed you, you loud whore, and one poem vanished. A whole people of neurotics, struggling to keep from being sane. And the only thing that would cure the neurosis would be your murder. Simple as that. I mean if I murdered you, then other white people would begin to understand me. You understand? No. I guess not. If Bessie Smith had killed some white people she wouldn't have needed that music. She could have talked very straight and plain about the world. No metaphors. No grunts. No wiggles in the dark of her soul. Just straight two and two are four. Money. Power. Luxury. Like that. All of them. Crazy niggers turning their backs on sanity. When all it needs is that simple act. Murder. Just murder! Would make us all sane.

[*Suddenly weary*]

Ahhh. Shit. But who needs it? I'd rather be a fool. Insane. Safe with my words, and no deaths, and clean, hard thoughts, urging me to new conquests. My people's madness. Hah! That's a laugh. My people. They don't need me to claim them. They got legs and arms of their own. Personal insanities. Mirrors. They don't need all those words. They don't need any defense. But listen, though, one more thing. And you tell this to your father, who's probably the kind of man who needs to know at once. So he can plan ahead. Tell him not to preach so much rationalism and cold logic to these niggers. Let them alone. Let them sing curses at you in code and see your filth as simple lack of style. Don't make the mistake, through some irresponsible surge of Christian charity, of talking too much about the advantages of Western rationalism, or the great intellectual legacy of the white man, or maybe they'll begin to listen. And then, maybe one day, you'll find they actually do understand exactly what you are talking about, all these fantasy people. All these blues people. And on that day, as sure as shit, when you really believe you can "accept" them into your fold, as half-white trusties late of the subject peoples. With no more blues, except the very old ones, and not a watermelon in sight, the great missionary heart will have triumphed, and all of those ex-coons will be stand-up Western men, with eyes for clean hard useful lives, sober, pious and sane, and they'll murder you. They'll murder you, and have very rational explanations. Very much like your own. They'll cut your throats, and drag you out to the edge of your cities so the flesh can fall away from your bones, in sanitary isolation.

LULA.
  [*Her voice takes on a different, more businesslike quality*]
I've heard enough.

CLAY.
  [*Reaching for his books*]

I bet you have. I guess I better collect my stuff and get off this train. Looks like we won't be acting out that little pageant you outlined before.

LULA.   No. We won't. You're right about that, at least.
   [*She turns to look quickly around the rest of the car*]
All right!
   [*The others respond*]

CLAY.
   [*Bending across the girl to retrieve his belongings*]
Sorry, baby, I don't think we could make it.
   [*As he is bending over her, the girl brings up a small knife and plunges it into* CLAY'*s chest. Twice. He slumps across her knees, his mouth working stupidly*]

LULA.   Sorry is right.
   [*Turning to the others in the car who have already gotten up from their seats*]
Sorry is the rightest thing you've said. Get this man off me! Hurry, now!
   [*The others come and drag* CLAY'*s body down the aisle*]
Open the door and throw his body out.
   [*They throw him off*]
And all of you get off at the next stop.
   [LULA *busies herself straightening her things. Getting every-thing in order. She takes out a notebook and makes a quick scribbling note. Drops it in her bag. The train apparently stops and all the others get off, leaving her alone in the coach.*

   Very soon a young Negro of about twenty comes into the coach, with a couple of books under his arm. He sits a few seats in back of LULA. *When he is seated she turns and gives him a long slow look. He looks up from his book and drops the book on his lap. Then an old Negro conductor comes into the car, doing a sort of restrained soft shoe, and half mumbling the words of some song. He looks at the young man, briefly, with a quick greeting*]

CONDUCTOR. Hey, brother!

YOUNG MAN. Hey.
[*The conductor continues down the aisle with his little dance and the mumbled song.* LULA *turns to stare at him and follows his movements down the aisle. The conductor tips his hat when he reaches her seat, and continues out the car*]

Curtain

67653
822.91
Jon